Percussion

Wendy Lynch

Heinemann
LIBRARY

www.heinemann.co.uk/library

Visit our website to find out more information about **Heinemann Library** books.

To order:

 Phone ++44 (0)1865 888066

 Send a fax to ++44 (0)1865 314091

 Visit the Heinemann Bookshop at www.heinemann.co.uk/library to browse our catalogue and order online.

First published in Great Britain by Heinemann Library, Halley Court, Jordan Hill, Oxford OX2 8EJ, a division of Reed Educational and Professional Publishing Ltd. Heinemann is a registered trademark of Reed Educational & Professional Publishing Ltd.

OXFORD MELBOURNE AUCKLAND JOHANNESBURG BLANTYRE
GABORONE IBADAN PORTSMOUTH NH (USA) CHICAGO

Designed by Visual Image
Illustration by Jane Watkins
Originated by Dot Gradations
Printed and bound in South China

ISBN 0 431 12903 7

05 04 03 02 01
10 9 8 7 6 5 4 3 2 1

British Library Cataloguing in Publication Data

Lynch, Wendy
  Percussion. – (Musical instruments)
  1. Percussion instruments – Juvenile literature
  I. Title
  786.8

Acknowledgements

The publishers would like to thank the following for permission to reproduce photographs: Corbis p21, Gareth Boden pp16, 24, 28, 29, Lebrecht collection pp11 (G Salter), 14 (Chris Stock), 19 (Chris Stock), Magnum (Ian Berry) p22, Photodisc pp6, 7, 12, Pictor pp4, 15, 20, Redferns pp8 (Andrew Lepley), 13 (David Redfern), 25 (David Redfern), 26 (Leon Morris), 27 (Mick Hutson), Rex p5, Robert Harding p23, Sally Greenhill pp17, 18, Travel Ink (David Toase) p9.

Cover photograph reproduced with permission of Photodisc.

Every effort has been made to contact copyright holders of any material reproduced in this book. Any omissions will be rectified in subsequent printings if notice is given to the Publisher.

Any words appearing in the text in bold, **like this**, are explained in the Glossary.

Contents

Making music together

There are many musical instruments in the world. Each instrument makes a different sound. We can make music together by playing these instruments in a band or an **orchestra**.

Bands and orchestras are made up of different groups of instruments. One of these groups is called percussion. In this steel band everyone is playing a percussion instrument.

What are percussion instruments?

Here you can see many different percussion instruments. They all make very different sounds. Drums beat, cymbals crash, and tambourines jingle.

rhythm sticks

triangle

snare drum

tambourine

You bang, shake or scrape percussion instruments to make a sound. They are made of strong material like gold, steel, bronze and wood.

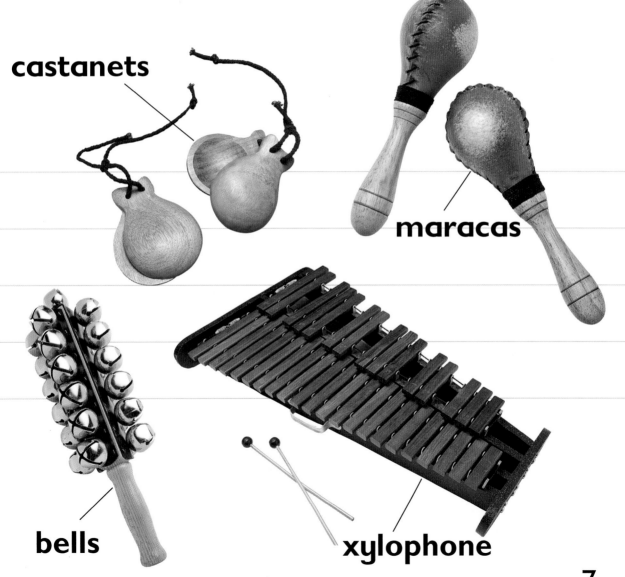

castanets

maracas

bells

xylophone

The drum

These are bongo drums. You tap them with your fingers or with your hands. You can make patterns of long or short sounds. This pattern is called a **rhythm**.

You can also play the drum with other instruments in a band or an **orchestra**. The drums play the rhythm for the other instruments in the orchestra or band.

How the sound is made

You strike the top of the drum to make a sound. This makes the air inside the drum move up and down. This movement is called **vibration**. When air vibrates, it makes a sound.

When the two metal discs of the cymbal crash into each other, it makes the metal vibrate. Big vibrations make a loud sound. Small vibrations make a soft sound.

Making a noise

The top of the drum is called the head. It is made of skin or plastic. Some drums make the same sound all the time. You can change the sound in others.

A sound can be high or low. This is called **pitch**. You press a pedal to change pitch for some drums. You **tighten** screws to change pitch for others.

Types of drum

Not all drums are the same. The bass drum plays the lowest and loudest notes. The **snare drum** has wires under the skin which rattle when you hit the drum.

You make steel drums from oil drums. You hit the top in different places to change the sound. They sound very different from other drums.

Triangle and xylophone

The triangle is a percussion instrument. You tap the triangle with a beater to make a high, tinkling sound. The note you play on the triangle is always the same.

The xylophone has wooden bars. Each bar plays a different note. These ring when you tap them with a beater. Some xylophones have a **hollow** wooden sound box under the bars.

Percussion section

In school you may play some other percussion instruments. You may play the chimes, the tambourine and the **rhythm** sticks.

Some percussion instruments are untuned. This means that they make the same sound all the time like the triangle. Other percussion instruments are tuned like tubular bells.

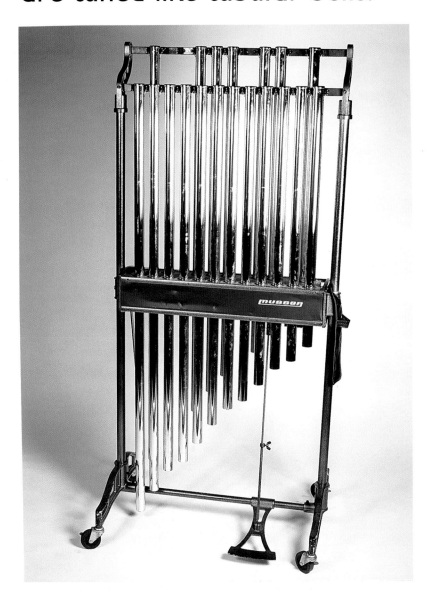

The wider family

Castanets have two pieces of wood tied on a cord. You click the wood together to make a sound. Castanets are used in Spain to make a **rhythm** for Spanish dancing.

The tambourine has small metal discs in its side. You hold the tambourine in your hand. When you shake the tambourine, you can hear the discs jingle.

Around the world

You can find percussion instruments all over the world. The kalungu or talking drum is from Africa. You can hear this drum across long distances and through forests.

The bonang is a set of gongs. It comes from Indonesia. You can hear the bonang and other percussion instruments in a **gamelan orchestra**.

Famous musicians and composers

A **composer** called Haydn wrote the Surprise Symphony. The surprise comes when you hear the very loud beat of the drum after some quiet music. People jump when they hear it.

Today you can hear Evelyn Glennie play percussion instruments. Evelyn is deaf. She can feel the **vibration** of the music as she plays.

New music

You can hear percussion instruments in **jazz** and **rock bands** today. The drum kit is important in **pop music**. It plays the beat. This helps people to dance in time to the music.

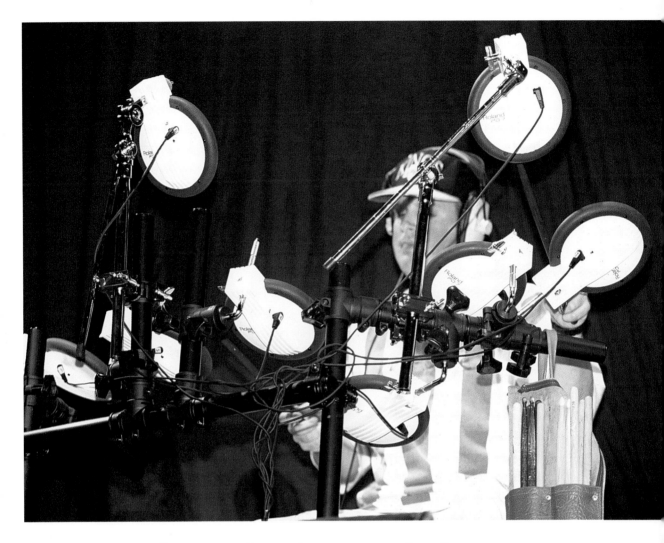

You can also make the sound of a drum with an electronic drum kit. You hit the pad of the drum. This sends a **pulse** to a control unit. This control unit makes the sound of the drum.

Sound activity

You can make your own percussion instruments. Put some rice in an empty yoghurt pot. Put another empty yoghurt pot on top of it and tape them together. Shake your shaker!

You can make a xylophone. Put six bottles or glasses in a line. Put different amounts of water in each bottle. Tap the bottles with a stick or wooden spoon.

Thinking about percussion

You can find the answers to all of these questions in this book.

1. How do you play percussion instruments?

2. Which drum plays the lowest, loudest notes?

3. What is the difference between a tuned and untuned percussion instrument?

4. What is a kalungu?

Glossary

composer person who writes new music

gamelan orchestra orchestra you can hear in Indonesia

hollow empty inside

jazz old style of music from America that is often made up as it is played

orchestra large group of musicians who play their musical instruments together
You say *or-kes-tra*

pitch the highness or lowness of a sound or musical note

pop music music of the last fifty years. A lot of people like this music.

pulse single beat

rhythm repeated beats or sounds that make a pattern
You say *rith-um*

rock bands group of musicians who play a kind of pop music with a strong beat

snare drum drum with strings or wires stretched across it

tighten to make something tighter or more close fitting

vibrate move up or down or from side to side very quickly

Index

HFL version

Titles in the *Musical Instuments* series include:

Hardback   0 431 12900 2

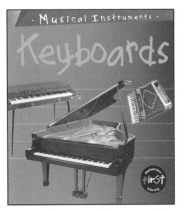

Hardback   0 431 12904 5

Hardback   0 431 12903 7

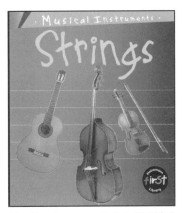

Hardback   0 431 12902 9

Hardback   0 431 12901 0

Find out about the other titles in this series on our website www.heinemann.co.uk/library